Thanks for All Your Help Matt.

Sandy Thompson

ONE IN A BILLION

Xploring the New World of China

Sandy Thompson

Photographs by
Chien-min Chung

Foreword by
Tom Peters

pH **powerHouse Books** New York, NY

Contents

Foreword

I have always believed that there are three pillars of excellent enterprise: extraordinary people, extraordinary products, and extraordinary customer experiences. To construct those pillars I suggest you fire up a love of adventure, make sure you have a serious presence or set down roots in China (the biggest customer pool in the world, indeed in the history of the world, growing at an unprecedented rate)...and study *One in a Billion*.

Sandy Thompson clearly understands that you cannot learn about customer habits, desires, or passions from behind a desk in general, and surely not in the Middle Kingdom. She knows that it is axiomatic that you have to get out and find these truths or create the trial hypotheses in the real world. She puts it well: "To truly understand China, we needed to open our minds to all the things we didn't know we didn't know."

While the idea of Xploring can be applied in every country and to every customer, the importance of this book right now is its concern with China. I've been a huge China advocate for two full decades, since I visited as a presidential exchange scholar in 1986, and Sandy is absolutely right—success in China depends on developing a fingertip feel for China, not rushing in, seduced by the size and siren call of the potential market as simply measured in dollars and quarterly earnings.

One in a Billion is a beautiful visual guide to what makes China special. (And as a "word guy," I reconfirm the truism that a picture is worth a thousand words—perhaps 10,000 in this case.) It gets us away from mumbling petty abstractions and into grappling with the look and feel and taste and touch of people's lives.

Take one quote at random...."You make money in China with two things: understanding and ambition. Ambition is easy to have. Understanding is much harder to get. This is why so many foreign companies find it hard." These few sentences alone could save billions of dollars for businesses trying to "crack" China.

Business is an affair of passion. That's the storyline of my professional life. Numbers are fine, but to succeed you need passion and emotion and empathy. And "time on the ground." That's what makes Sandy's insights so convincing, and her stories so compelling. She introduces us to a tremendous range of engaging and dynamic people doing what they do best: being themselves.

Following Sandy's lead will give you a great start. As *One in a Billion* shows us, the rewards can be great. And whatever happens, you'll have the chance to meet a billion or so wonderful people and hear some amazing, mind-blowing stories.

—Tom Peters

The Numbers Rush

5,000 years of history   Over **700** cities   Over **20,000** towns   **4** municipalities, **23** provinces, **7** regions   One official language with **7** dialects   **41** minority languages   Highest point Mt Everest, known as Mt. Qomolangma in China, at **8,850** meters above sea level   **9,571,000** square kilometers   **3,695,000** square miles   An estimated **1.3 billion** people   **123** people per square kilometer   Over **20%** of the world's population   **71%** aged between **15** and **64** years old   **33%** under the age of **21**   **672.7 million** men and **633.6 million** women   **265 million** citizens aged **14** and under   **99 million** citizens aged **65** and over   An estimated **30 million** homosexuals   Over **10,000** births per day   Average life expectancy of **72** years   **320 million** smokers   **200 million** people learning English   **450 million** people with a college degree   **70%** of the population nondenominational or atheist   The world's largest television market, with sales of over **30 million** sets in 2002   Over **111 million** Internet users at the end of 2005, **64%** on broadband   More than **64%** reported they spent less time watching TV and **67%** said they slept less   Cumulative GDP growth of **34.5%** since 1998   In 2004 China's GDP was **$US1.6 trillion**, the world's **7**th highest   **12%** of China's entire GDP is made up of exports to the US   **1%** of GDP is made up of exports to Wal-Mart   By 2010 China's GDP will exceed **$US2 trillion**   An estimated **3 million** millionaires and **1,000** billionaires   **Quadruple** growth in personal incomes over the last **20** years   City residents earn **31** times more than rural residents   An estimated **$US2 trillion** in savings accounts   **80 million** stock investors Over **60 million** Communist Party members   In 2002 **90 billion** text messages were sent, an average of **246 million** messages per day, on over **400 million** mobile phones   **500%** growth in American high-tech exports to China between 1990 and 1998   World's largest number of cable TV viewers   Domestic automotive manufacturing expected to surpass Japan's by 2015 **28%** of Silicon Valley's entrepreneurs are of Chinese origin   E-commerce revenues rose from **$US2.1 billion** in 2000 to **$US26 billion** in 2004   China attracts more direct foreign investment than any country except the US   **54%** of the Chinese population believes that China will be the most powerful country in the world within the next **5** years

Every time I met with new business clients in China they would introduce themselves by showing me statistics like these. As businesspeople, they were focused on the numbers and the massive potential for profit. Over a billion people, with almost 2 trillion US dollars in savings. The numbers are truly astonishing, but they are only half of the story.

China is a completely different world from the West. The history is different, the food is different, the culture is different, and the marketplace is different. Metric models from the West will only get you so far in China. They tell you nothing about who the people of China are.

This book is about the people who live, work, and play in China. Throw away the charts and graphs, put on a pair of walking shoes, and follow me. This is how you get to know a country.

—Sandy Thompson

To truly understand China, you need to Xplore.

Xploring is probably the oldest research technique ever used. Most companies seem to have forgotten about it, even though Xploring is far easier to conduct, more affordable, more insightful, and more effective than most other market research practices.

When Saatchi & Saatchi first arrived in China, we began in the most rational way possible. We encouraged our clients to invest in gathering knowledge. We looked for better, more insightful research. We invested our own money in focus groups to collect as much information as we could. We gathered numbers.

We quickly realized that recruiting respondents and taking them through a prepared question list would only give us the answers to the questions we knew how to ask.

To truly understand China, we needed to open our minds to all the things we didn't know we didn't know.

Xploring is based on a simple principle. If you want to understand how a lion hunts, you don't go to the zoo. You go to the jungle.

The team and I, frustrated with focus groups, decided to get on the road and go. We hired two drivers and a videographer. We left Beijing at 1 AM and started driving, not knowing whether our idea would work. But after Xploring for three weeks we managed to come back with a wealth of information that we would never have found in a laboratory.

Saatchi & Saatchi has now covered over 50,000km in China with backpacks and sneakers.

That's the equivalent of twice around the planet, by van, boat, and train.

We could have hired a research company or a consulting firm to present us with a stack of notes on the Chinese market. But all we would have gained is knowledge. What we sought was an understanding.

While Xploring we met children, parents, and grandparents. We met gas station attendants with ambitions to own their own business. We met children who aspired to learn English, not so they could study abroad, but so that they could make China stronger in the world market. We spent time with people who have been forced to move from their homes and close their businesses because of the flooding of the Yangtze, but who are happy about the change and the progress it means for their country. There are children with ambitions to keep China clean. There are teenagers who believe in the power of market communism over democracy. There are old men who believe today's China is a woman's world. And there are young students who believe the future of the world's economy is firmly in the hands of China.

In our travels we sat down and talked with thousands of individuals in China.

The people you will discover on the following pages are a small sample of those we met and spent time with. Some we met for only a minute or two at a street corner. Some we spoke to for hours over a cup of coffee or tea, or while we helped them cook dinner in their homes.

To Xplore, you need to have the courage to approach strangers and ask the dumb questions. You need to realize that the statistics mean nothing and that you know nothing. An Xplorer needs to be fearless.

To be a successful Xplorer in China you need to start from scratch. You need to take the time to understand China, its people and their motivations. The people of China have their hopes and dreams firmly set on their country's future. They have no desire to look back.

As one young student told us, "Nothing can stop you from going forward if you have confidence. Right now, China has more confidence than any other country in the world."

The "numbers" of China have seduced many successful and intelligent businesspeople from around the world.

They have been lured to the shores of China by the prospect of fame, fortune, and double-digit growth: easy growth within the world's largest developing market. China is a country that has emerged from years of poverty and repression to become a modern market economy.

The numbers have commanded the world's attention. The greater the numbers, the more potential there is and the more sales. More sales mean more bonuses, more shoes in the closet, more square feet to live in, more five-star holidays, and hope of an earlier, more lavish retirement.

China is a breeding ground for numbers euphoria.

The world's best marketing people take one look at the Chinese market and they get giddy. "It's a gorilla of a country," they say. There are 1.3 billion people, with over 3,000,000 millionaires and 1,000 billionaires. It is estimated that there are over 2 trillion US dollars in Chinese savings accounts. And there's no way to accurately estimate the millions and millions of dollars hidden under mattresses, behind sofas, or in boxes pushed under beds.

Many believe that China's growth has been driven through exports, powered by the world's largest labor force. On the contrary, 95 percent of China's growth in the last two years has been generated by domestic demand.

Chinese desire has grown with Chinese wealth. In Mao's days people dreamed about the "four musts": a bicycle, radio, watch, and sewing machine. Under Deng Xiaoping people began acquiring the "eight bigs": a color television, fridge, stereo, camera, motorcycle, suite of furniture, washing machine, and electric fan. Today there are no "four musts" and no "eight bigs." People no longer number their desires.

There are a lot of people in China and a lot of money to be spent on shampoos, clothes, cars, houses, insurance, dish detergents, TVs, video games, travel, and electronic gadgets. Billions of dollars will be spent on the latest sneakers, children's educations, mobile phones, and fast food.

The Chinese are spending these days. The challenge is to get them to spend their billions on what you are selling.

Let's be clear. It's not easy. Gaining global market share in the world's largest emerging market is more difficult than anyone imagined.

Once upon a time, success in China could be found simply by showing up. The first wave of foreign investment came into China on the promise of a huge market. Many assumed that building brand awareness would be sufficient. For a few years it was possible to make inroads with a good distribution network and a big advertising budget. Brands like Coca-Cola, Motorola, IBM, and Procter & Gamble dug in this way, by spending billions of dollars on infrastructure, labor, and marketing.

Motorola invested huge sums in China and quickly gained a substantial market share. Between 2002 and 2003, Chinese phone vendors increased their capacity from 30 million handsets to well over 170 million. Motorola expected competition from global rivals such as Nokia and Ericsson, but no one predicted a challenge from local brands. Local manufacturers like TCL and Ningbo Bird made handsets that catered to local tastes with products that ran the gamut from conservative to kitschy. Local phones came in a range of colors, and some were inlaid with diamonds long before Paris Hilton decorated hers. Motorola and Nokia continue to lead the handset market in China, but TCL and Ningbo Bird are providing strong competition.

Procter & Gamble entered the Chinese market expecting that they would compete solely with other foreign brands. But today some of their toughest competition comes from local brands manufactured in China, by Chinese, for Chinese. The good news is Procter & Gamble has recognized the changing environment and has adapted its strategies, product offering, and geographic expansions.

In China, relying on deep pockets to maintain brand profile can be a dangerous game.

Motorola and Procter & Gamble have succeeded, but plenty of other international brands charged into China and spent billions of dollars to gain quick market share and recognition, only to find themselves struggling.

The key to being successful in China, no matter your resources, is an understanding of the people. Many companies forget that while there might be 1.3 billion potential customers, there are also 1.3 billion people with dreams, ambitions, and desires of their own. There are 1.3 billion people who see their country with a pride and ambition unrivaled by any other in the world. There are 1.3 billion people who you have little hope of winning over unless you can find a strong point of connection.

To be successful in China, you need China to fall in love with you.

Though the people of China might respect your size, your past successes, and your global reputation, you need the people of China to completely fall in love with your brand and to desire you beyond reason.

As an Xplorer you must ignore the numbers and instead take the time to try and understand the people. You must acknowledge their dreams, their motivations, their desires, and their lives. In doing so, you give people a reason to love you back.

4. The Power of Spirit

Many countries have gone from feeling strong, powerful, and dominant to fearful and paranoid.

They have stopped worrying about the future, and they fear the present.

Newspapers are depressing, and the evening news sends people to bed with a head full of questions and concerns. No one knows whether to spend for the moment or save for the future. They don't know whether to support their government or to oppose them. They don't know whether to enjoy life or to prepare for the worst.

But in one corner of the earth, there are billions of people whose spirit is growing. These people believe in their future, in their government, in their businesses, and in themselves.

There are some in China who are deeply troubled by both government and private industry corruption. Like the West, there is concern over the ever-increasing wage gap between the rich in the

There are more people coming to China now.
More people who are interested in seeing what we have achieved.
More people who are afraid of what we will achieve. "

" **The most precious thing in China right now is our sprit.**
With it we can move mountains. "

city and the rest of the population who are struggling to survive in the country. There is concern about increasing rates of unemployment and divorce.

But in China, optimism runs high. An inexperienced Xplorer might look at a country like China and label it as being backward, because of its lack of space, air-conditioned homes, shopping malls, five-star restaurants, and Starbucks cafés. Some short-sighted Western businessmen we traveled with saw this lack of luxury as inhuman.

The people of China are far-sighted; they don't see a lack of luxury, but room for growth. They see the changes occurring in China and are proud of where their country is going. They see new roads being built. They see new apartment blocks being constructed. They see department stores full of electronic equipment. They see change.

They feel the growing strength of China. They have an abundance of spirit. They believe they have the power to succeed beyond all imagination.

" **We do everything for our country not because it is our duty,** but because we love China. It is our home. "

"China's future will be stronger
than any Western country's because we believe.
In our people and in our dreams."

"We are not emerging.
We have emerged."

China is like a newborn cow.
We have no fear of the tiger.

" Our history is old.
But our future is young. **"**

"Even though you fail sometimes, there are always ways to get ahead. **With confidence you can do everything.**"

❝ Because we are changing so quickly there is a need for China to preserve its traditional culture. **❞**

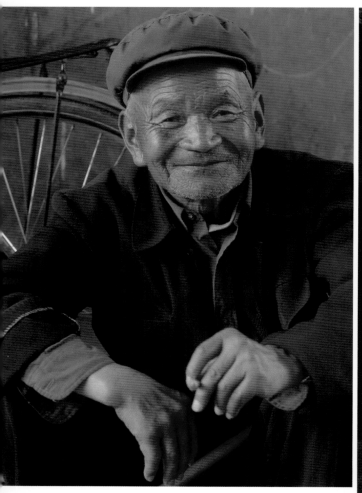

❝ I smile so much because I am happy. China is happy. If I had one wish it would be for everyone to be as happy as I am. **❞**

Flooding the Yangtze

One day you're told to move house. You have to leave the home that your mother and father lived in and left to you. You also have to close down your business. Your income is gone overnight, as is the business you built up over many years. It's the only business you know.

You will be paid a nominal fee for your home. But you will be paid nothing for your shop, your store, or your livelihood. You are told to start over.

Many people along the Yangtze faced this situation. Many of them saw their homes and businesses flooded. They were forced to move. They had to buy new houses and businesses, if they could afford them.

As Xplorers, we were expecting to see anger and frustration. Some people were angry, but we were surprised at how many people saw the change as positive.

As one man told us: "Change is good. It means a bigger home and maybe if I am lucky, more money. Everything is new. And while I may have to start over, I have the chance to build something bigger, and to create a better life than I had before."

5. The Key to Their Success

I wish I could catch all the Chinese misses and put them back in the net.

The statistics suggest that China will most likely be successful.

They tell us that growth is strong and that many foreign companies have a chance of hitting the jackpot and capturing the pocketbooks of the world's largest national population.

But numbers ignore the individual. Xploring introduced us to the ambition of the individual, something not even hinted at in the statistics.

China is not waiting for the world to come to them. They are not waiting for foreign support or goods, or a strong labor force to fuel their export business. The people of China are not waiting for anything or anyone.

The people of China have their own ambitions and they dream big.

We often found ourselves Xploring muddy villages, talking to young teens whose ambitions exceeded our own. Their dreams of making it were not constrained by where they were starting from. These were not the children of privileged families. Often their parents left them as infants in the care of grandparents, so that they could go in search of additional income to send their child to school.

Though these children had little then, they believed that they could have it all tomorrow.

“ In Hong Kong it's going to take another 20 or 30 years
for another Li Ka-Shing to come along.
**But in China everybody wants to be
Li Ka-Shing in 5 years. ,,**

Why not? China is a land of unlimited possibilities. One of the world's top computer companies, Lenovo Computers, is 100 percent Chinese. Lenovo began life as Legend computers, which was the top-selling computer brand in China and in most of the Asia Pacific region between 1997 and 2003, outselling IBM, Dell, or HP.

In 2004, Lenovo bought IBM's worldwide personal computer hardware business for US$650 million. They are now selling personal computers back into the United States, taking the challenge to Dell and Hewlett Packard on their home turf.

There's a piano company on the Pearl River that started life humbly in 1956 and is now one of the world's largest piano manufacturers. It employs over 4,000 people and has the capacity to produce over 100,000 pianos a year, which it exports around the world.

Li Ning Sports Group was founded by Li Ning, well known in China as the "Prince of Gymnastics." In 2002, his Sports Group was generating as much revenue in China as Nike or adidas. A Li Ning product was being sold every ten seconds.

Like Li Ning, many of the people in China have huge ambitions that dwarf any obstacles they might face.

We met many people who are not waiting to consume global brands, but instead plan to create their own. This is a country whose people truly believe that nothing is impossible.

"You have to be strong in China. But in being strong, China is stronger. And if China is stronger we all benefit."

“ Before, you blamed the government for being poor.
Now, if you are poor, it's your fault.,,

❝ If you look hard enough there are only opportunities.
People make money everywhere, just open your eyes. ❞

Musicians in Wuhan

One night in Wuhan, we were serenaded by street musicians. They played songs for 10 yuan (US$1.25).* We were amazed at how good they were.

They told us that they used to be part of a troupe of musicians in China. When the troupe lost its government funding they were laid off. The rice they ate and the roof over their head was taken away overnight.

They weren't bitter, angry, or depressed. They were happy. It meant that China was moving forward. China was encouraging people to find their own way instead of depending on others.

As one performer told us, "Free competition teaches us to find and fight for our own position in society. You either have to be the best player on the stage or you have to find a different audience. It is the only way to succeed."

*At a 1 : .1247 exchange, current as of April 2006.

> **"**It is getting easier for foreign companies to come into China. China is developing, so naturally we choose a better life. But they (foreigners) should also know it is easier to run a business now. Easier to earn our own money. **"**

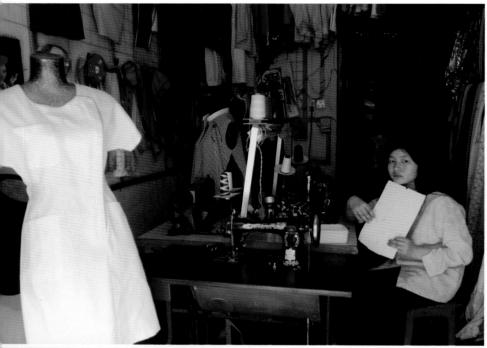

> **"**When you are working hard you will inspire others. We never give up. We are proving to the world that we are good. **"**

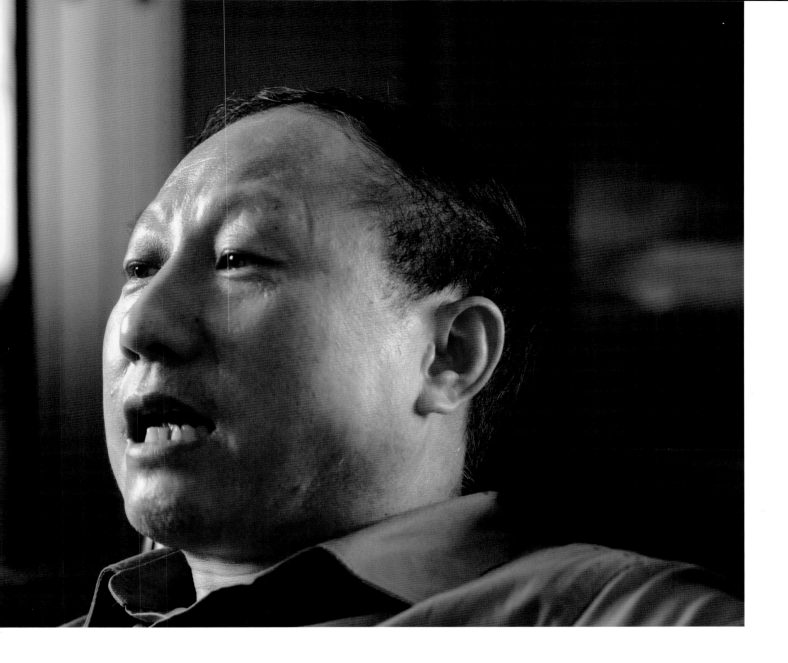

" You make money in China with two things: understanding and ambition. Ambition is easy to have. Understanding is much harder to get. This is why so many foreign companies find it hard. "

The Gas Station Attendant

She had style. We thought she might be an artist, musician, or writer. Instead, she was a gas station attendant. She was also one of the smartest, most articulate people we met. We spent over an hour with her, discussing the future of China and the challenges faced by overseas marketers.

She summed it up this way, "When it comes to foreign companies coming into China it's going to be like the race between the tortoise and the hare. The arrogant hare might just end up losing to what he thinks is a slow-moving tortoise."

" With self-belief you can find success. China has self-belief. "

" China will keep improving even though I have all the things I want. "

6. Face Value

Xplorers don't barge into people's lives uninvited and start asking questions.

Xploring is about giving and receiving. As a white woman in China, people were as curious about me as I was about them.

We learned very quickly that if we wanted people to be open with us, we needed to be open with them. A willingness to share knowledge with someone shows that you respect them and trust them to use the knowledge wisely. In China respect is extremely important.

The idea of "face" exists in almost every culture of the world, but in Asia it is paramount. Face drives society. It drives business and politics. It can motivate people or destroy them. It has the power to bind people together and it can also tear them apart. Understanding face is key to being successful in China.

In China, face exists in one's mind, not in words. It drives what individuals do and how they do it.

华中理工大学船海系
华都轮船总公司造船厂
一九九六年四月

"Today in China you can choose to do nothing or to do something.
The strong do something. „

China has always been a society guided with the collective group in mind. As such, the individual's status and significance is often defined by their role within a community.

The fear of losing face is huge. We spoke to many men who had recently lost their jobs. When a man loses his job it is often seen as a direct reflection of his capability and worth. Losing one's job is demoralizing. As a result, many of the unemployed men we met were immobilized, and were struggling to find another job. Some were content to stay home and become househusbands. They could play mahjongg into the wee hours of the morning instead of having to face the task of finding work.

Women who were laid off seemed to cope much better. While their jobs were important in terms of making a family contribution, they didn't regard their job as a reflection of their ability or worth. As a result, many of the women we spoke to didn't feel a loss of face when their job was taken away from them. Many women saw this as an opportunity to break free from their job and find a career.

Many of the women in China are gaining face while men are losing face.

Gaining face is not easy. But like money, once you have face, it is easier to gain more. Face is usually based on one's social status, credibility, reputation, and social connections. The more face you have,

"The Olympics in 2008 will be the best Olympics ever because we believe. Because we are Chinese we will look good to the world. They will respect us."

" I will be happy if my future wife makes more money than me. She can pay all my expenses. She just can't tell anyone. "

the better others will treat you. Because your face is determined by others' attitudes towards you, face is difficult to gain. It takes time and hard work.

We spoke to young engaged men who worked day and night in order to afford a decent wedding ceremony. We met a family who temporarily rented a nicer home with months and months of salary purely to impress an overseas guest. We met parents who spent up to 70 percent of their income on their five-year-old child to pay for his piano lessons, computer, and branded clothes.

Giving face involves making a person look good in front of others. This sounds easy, but mastering the skill of giving face requires a significant level of interpersonal sensitivities. Some foreigners don't have the delicacy for it.

Face anywhere in the world is like a mask: it is not always a true reflection of fact. What people might say in a focus group or on the street is not necessarily how they might feel. As a result we need to dig much deeper than words. We need to be aware of people's motivations and sensitivities. Most importantly, we need to understand how to make people feel good about themselves, irrespective of culture.

“ I think people in the old days were taught to help each other. But now everyone can make money. Everyone now works for his or her own benefit. ”

“ After dinner I keep reading, working on the computer, and learning English. Otherwise I will be lagging behind the world too much and have no idea what my child is doing. ”

"High unemployment in China has been very good for women. We use to just have a job.

Now we have the opportunity to find a career."

Respect and Marriage

We met her and asked if we could see her home. We wanted to meet her husband, her son, and her parents. When we got there, her father and son were watching cartoons on television. Over a few glasses of warm Pepsi, with her grandmother sitting behind the sofa on a small bed, our new friend and her husband spoke about their relationship.

He had been unemployed for some time, and she was the primary income earner, working as a travel agent. Her husband was very proud of her and what she had achieved. It was much harder for him to earn a living now with rising unemployment. We asked her about her relationship with her husband and she told us it was good. He was a good father and he loved their son very much. He took care of their son while she was at work, and made sure he got to school and that he ate properly.

Quite unexpectedly she told us how he sometimes disappeared for days. He told her that he was playing mahjongg with his friends. She knew it wasn't true. He knew she knew it wasn't true. Now we knew. The grandmother stared at her shoes. The grandfather continued watching Tom and Jerry.

As the conversation continued, with him praising her intelligence, her beauty, her patience, we realized she no longer loved him. But she respected him.

She later told us, "A husband deserves your respect. But your boyfriend gets your love." She went on to say, "While your husband may be the one who loves you; your boyfriend is the one you love."

Through Xploring, we came to understand that for many of the husbands and wives we met, love and respect didn't always coexist.

For now this woman continues to give her husband face, but when she no longer respects him, she will take it away.

7. More than Half the Sky

Xploring is a focused approach to research. As an Xplorer, you need to have a goal in mind and a set of questions you want answered.

Focus groups use discussion guides, and we used them too. But unlike focus groups, we weren't bound by time. We let conversation flow naturally, allowing people to take us where they wanted.

Our earliest Xplorations were focused on women. Many traditional thinkers in China believe that women were created for men, or belong to men. A woman's role was to be a daughter, wife, or mother. Their family was their world. They were educated to be tender, understanding, supportive, subservient, devoted, and loyal. A great-grandmother we met told us: "If a woman marries a dog she should follow that dog. If she marries a chicken she should follow that chicken."

That was a long time ago. After the Communist Party consolidated their leadership in China in the late 1940s, equality became a reality. Rich and poor, working class and elite, men and women: everyone was at the same level, and everyone was

"A woman with a career but no family is a successful woman. But a woman with only a family and no career is not a complete woman."

called upon to participate in the construction of a socialist society.

Every member of society was given a job and paid equally. For the first time, a woman shared the financial responsibility for her family with her husband.

One of our Xplorers, Heidi, explained to us that twenty years ago her mother used to work as an accountant, earning 35,000 yuan (US$4,364.50) a year. Her father, an established doctor, only earned 30,000 yuan (US$3,741.00) a year. It had never occurred to her that her father's career was more important than her mother's or vice versa. They were equal. Both were responsible for the financial status of the family.

Women in China achieved financial equality with men long before so-called progressive countries like the United States or the United Kingdom. For a long time now, the women of China have stood beside men in the hope of building a great nation.

In Western cultures, a woman who has managed to balance her family with her career is a Superwoman. The Superwoman is an extraordinary creature that can command attention in a boardroom while raising loving, well-behaved children at home.

Many of the women in China are already Superwomen. For decades women in China did not have a choice between family and career. Women had to work for financial and social reasons. For a sense of duty and responsibility they had to take care of their family.

Today, women in China are fighting for something different. As one woman told us, "In China, women are educated to be strong and financially independent. A woman's value is in being a wife, a mother, and a decent salary earner. She must know how to do her job and she must be devoted to her family."

While Western women seek a balance between career and family, many Chinese women have

moved beyond it. Today the women of China are seeking mental independence.

Some say that Chinese women want a career at the expense of family. Others disagree. One young woman told us: "A woman with a career but no family is a successful woman. But a woman with only a family and no career is not a complete woman."

The women of China don't want to become men. They have no desire to achieve success by male standards: using brashness, demanding respect, and driven by a desire to fuel their own egos. The women in China are happy being women and they plan to succeed with their femininity intact.

The ideal woman is adaptable, an equal to any man, well educated, and goal oriented. At the same time she believes in being a woman, and she uses her intelligence and intuition to manage, not her ego.

A strong and successful woman thinks first with her heart and then with her head.

"Her mother is off working in Beijing.
She and I live together now and I cook for her.
Her mother sends us money for her food and school. "

> Her mother hasn't seen her since she was first born. She left her so she can give to her. To make money so she can live a better life than we do.

“Raising a kid is like working on a project.
You have a goal to achieve and your goal is to make him or her into a successful person. „

"**I am the whole sky, so I want to fly.**
Fly as high as an eagle, all the while keeping the beauty of a butterfly. "

Chinese Mothers

We met many mothers while Xploring, as we were naturally drawn to children. After a while our photographer understood that whenever a child was nearby, our progress would be halted while we sat and chatted with them. While Chinese mothers always appeared affectionate and attentive with their kids, we began to sense that being a mother was as much a career to these women as the career they paid the rent with.

We asked them: "What makes a successful mother in China? How do you know if you are a good mother or not?"

I measure my success as a mom by my children's happiness, their ability to give, and their confidence. In China many of the mothers measured their success quite differently. To them a successful mother was one who succeeded in bringing up a competitive achiever, an achiever that they themselves dream and aspire to be.

As one young mother told us, "Being a mother is not about good or bad, it is about success or failure."

Another told us, "If she turns out to be ordinary I shouldn't have given birth to her in the first place. Raising a child is like working on a project. You have a goal to achieve."

For Chinese moms, kids are not just kids. Kids are a continuance of their life: vessels for their hopes and dreams. They are the assurance that whatever they don't achieve in this life, their kids will.

There is one universal truth that we witnessed over and over again. All Chinese mothers, regardless of their ambition, love their children completely.

" I will give her everything and deprive her of nothing. "

Marriage

We asked many of the women we met what they expected to be the highlight of their life. A great many told us it would be their wedding day.

"It will be my day. I want to have it in a big concert hall with thousands of people watching. I won't know them all but that won't matter. It will be a big show: a fashion show for all the clothes I design myself with the theme of Oriental Beauty. A concert show for my husband. We will be in the center of the stage, in the middle of the spotlight, the focus of attention for everyone watching. Our guests will be there to share and to celebrate the moment, its glamour and its success. There will be envy everywhere. I will be beautiful."

❝ I dare to think. I dare to do. When I get old I don't want any regrets. ❞

My children will improve my life. With them I will drive a better car and I will own my own house. Then I want to go traveling. I might go to the southern shore. If they can help me afford to go to foreign countries then I will go to Singapore or Japan. They make me happy today and they will make me happy into my old age.

Being a mother isn't about good or bad.
It is about success or failure.

The days when men were men and women were women are long gone.

It used to be that after a hard day's work, a man would come home, put his feet up, smoke a cigarette, and wait for his loving wife to finish preparing his dinner.

Children no longer see their father as the family's sole provider or the protector that holds it together. Men no longer rule the household. Once upon a time, women were to obey their fathers first, their husbands upon marriage, and their sons once widowed, but not any more.

A man's home is no longer his castle.

The winds have changed, and men have changed.

Women are getting stronger. While some men accept and admire this in their mothers and sisters, most don't want to deal with it in a wife.

Many men in China are finding it hard to find a wife. Recent reports have indicated that there are over 70 million single men in China of marriageable age. Some blame the one child policy and the belief that a male child is more valuable than a female, while others blame women and their desire to have a career over family.

Maybe the shortage of women is the reason why many men in China are beginning to pamper themselves a bit more. Spa treatments, designer clothes, and luxury cars are fighting for their attention and winning.

The more time we spent with the men of China the more we realized that they don't have it easy.

" I wouldn't look like I minded, but there would still be a feeling of insecurity in my mind if my wife earned more money than I did. "

Women are becoming stronger and they are changing the rules of the game. Today's generation of men can no longer rely on their fathers or grandfathers as role models. The masculinity of yesterday won't work in the China of today.

The winds have changed. Men must find new ways to define who they are, what they offer to society and the roles they play at work, at home with their wives, their girlfriends, and their families.

" I would rather be a boy than a girl. Girls are demanding. They want answers for everything. Boys are easygoing. Besides what if I am ugly as a girl? "

> **In a crisis a man must pretend to be cool and calm.**
> **We have to. We have no choice.**

“ Looks are very important. Even if you are
not strong you must always look strong. ”

“ Male status is deteriorating.
Women don't rely on us anymore. ”

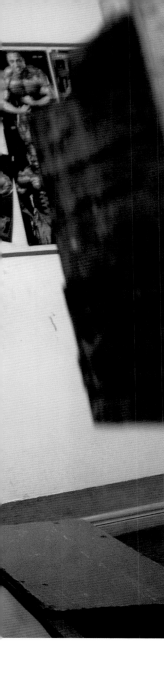

Sometimes we have fun.

My wife now has friendships with other men. I feel uncomfortable with it, but there is little I can do.

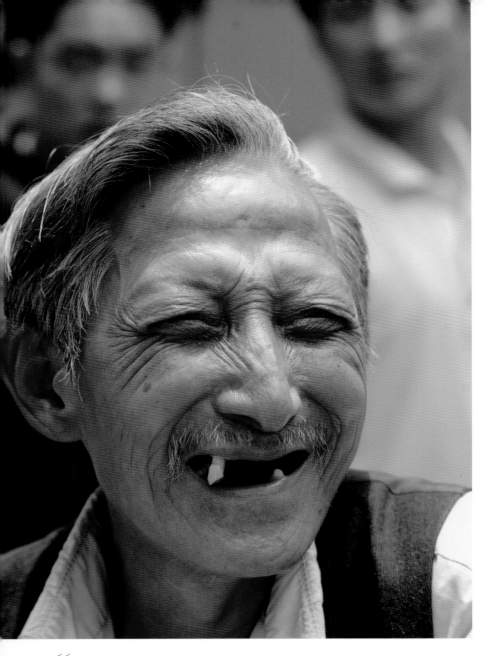

> ❝My father's life is different from mine.
> We have little in common.❞

"My father only thought of working hard for China.
Now we have more choices and more opportunities for the future. **"**

“The sky would fall if men were not around.”

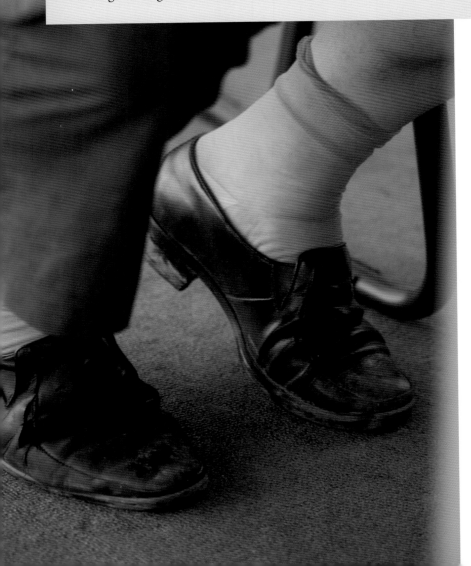

Men and Women

One day we met a man wearing women's stockings. He said, "China was a man's world. Today it's for women. They are the ones with all the chances. It's not easy for men these days. We're not sure what a man is supposed to be.

"Mao made men and women equal overnight. He gave women in China a head start over women elsewhere in the world when he proclaimed that women would have to hold up their half of the sky, just like men."

This man wishes he was a woman, because the China of the future is for women. Women drive change. While men may be the ones seeking glory, it is the women of China who make it strong.

❝I share more with my male friends than with my wife.**❞**

9. Fooled by Appearances

Being a teen anywhere in the world means you are going through confusing and exciting changes in your life.

Who you are is not who you want to be. Are you independent? Are you going to conform or do your own thing? Is adulthood the beginning of your freedom or the end of your security? Is this what you want, or only what you think you want?

All teens go through a period of self-realization and discovery where everything is frustrating, confusing, and difficult.

Chinese teens are no different. Like teens anywhere in the world, they are going through enormous changes. We found it hard to pin them down and even harder to understand them.

But in China there are a few other factors to consider.

First of all, this is the first generation to be born into the one-child policy. In 1979, the Chinese government, in an attempt to control its exploding population, restricted families to one child.

The vast majority of teens you meet in China today are the first generation to be raised in single child families.

We must also consider China's education system. It is evolving fast, giving kids opportunities that previous generations of teens did not have access to. They can choose to study in China, or to go abroad. If they are one of those fortunate students to surpass their peers in intensely competitive higher education examinations, they can choose their curriculum, their school, and their future.

Today's Chinese kids are much wealthier than the generation of teens before them. When you

“ I will learn English, and I will
become a Japanese pop star. ”

combine growing income levels with the one child policy, it follows that a large proportion of this generation of teens will want for nothing. The only fear is that their drive and ambition will suffer, because they have everything and have no reason to work hard. That is, except for the exceedingly competitive reality they will face in today's job market.

The world is smaller for these teens than it was for previous generations. We spent time in Internet cafés watching young girls speak English to their friends in Germany, or Japanese to their boyfriends in Tokyo. They read magazines, listen to music, and watch movies from every corner of the planet.

So while these teens are going through the same growing pains as every other teen in the world, there are some unique differences.

Will they be the generation to take China forward or will they be the downfall of a country on the verge of great things? For Chinese teens, there are not only the traditional rites of passage that all teens go through, but also the pressure of the economic, social, and political changes that their country is experiencing.

"I was born in a comparatively well-off family. But I know I can't rely on my parents for the rest of my life. I need to study and learn how to live on my own. As long as I keep working hard and grab my chance I believe that I will be successful. I have confidence in myself."

Left Alone

It was a wet day and the roads were bad. We took shelter at a village, where we met a nine-year-old boy. He had a fever and was suffering from a "running stomach"—or diarrhea. His parents had left the village long ago in search of work. His father worked in a factory in Chengdu and his mother was a maid in Beijing. They had left him on his own. His grandfather took care of him when he could. Other villagers made sure he ate and went to school. His parents hadn't forgotten him: they sent money to pay for his bills. They had been doing so since he was four.

He didn't mind not seeing his parents. "They work hard to make my life better, so I can go to school and grow up and get a good job."

“ We are proud of the fact that we are Chinese. Although some foreigners think we are not as good as them, I think the Chinese are able and confident. ”

“ Last October I was in London for one year. But now I am back. When I came back I could hardly recognize the buildings. There are many high and new buildings. It is good. ”

“ In the past China was powerful. Although there was a period of depression, China is getting better and better. As a Chinese I should try my best to make my country as powerful as before. ”

“ If I can run a school and train the next generation I consider that to be a good use of my knowledge. ”

"My parents don't like that we dress fashionably. But I explained to them that all kids in Japan dress like this, they are well off and the king of the house."

112

> "Even if I study abroad I would come back and work. I won't stay there. **Success is better here.**"

> "I think if you have a chance to use what you learn from another country to help the development of your country that's a good thing, a thing to be proud of. In the past our country did not have a chance to import foreign knowledge. Now we do."

"I am not sure where I will be in 5 years. Society keeps changing. I think I will have my own car, live in a European-style house, and be living my ideal life."

"I am lost. I feel like floating in the ocean."

"I want to run a gorgeous business that will benefit me. And China."

10. A Clean Start

“ When I grow up I hope we can drive cars without gas. Then we can breathe again. ”

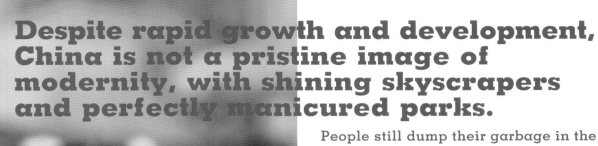

Despite rapid growth and development, China is not a pristine image of modernity, with shining skyscrapers and perfectly manicured parks.

People still dump their garbage in the streets, cars pollute the air, factories cloud the sky, and rivers run thick with waste.

China's size, population, and economic growth have put the environment at risk. China houses 1.3 billion people on a landmass not much larger than that of the United States. The Chinese government is very aware of the high environmental cost they might pay. Since the 1980s they have been working with organizations from all over the world to develop better manufacturing methods, better ways of minimizing waste, and have made efforts to meet world environmental standards. They are making progress, though not as fast as some might like.

As Xplorers, we talked to individuals, not corporations. We spent time with children whose fortunes are tied to the China of the future.

We watched people haphazardly drop their rice boxes over the side of boats floating up the Yangtze River. We witnessed old men habitually spitting into the streets as they walked with their barefoot grandchildren. We saw houses surrounded by years of waste, and children squatting on public sidewalks, defecating to the tune of Grandma's whistle. We saw broken bicycles, spilt garbage, dead animals on the banks of rivers, green haze emitted from local factories, and streets dense with exhaust fumes. All are common, depending on where you might be in China, and people mostly ignore it and go about their business.

At first glance we thought no one cared. But the more people we spoke to, the more we Xplored, the more we realized we were wrong.

People care. But many people in China don't understand how one person's change in behavior can solve the bigger problem. How do you convince Grandpa, who has spat on the street all his life, to stop? Will his stopping really make the streets cleaner?

How do you convince a mother to spend money on diapers for her child instead of letting her go in the street? How do you convince people to think twice about buying a car that will only add more fumes to the street when a car is such a potent symbol of success and progress?

You can't. People don't change overnight and habits are not easily broken. But the people of China will learn through their schools, through government funded programs and through their children. It will just take time.

Just because the people of China will not change quickly does not mean they don't appreciate companies who take the environment into consideration. We spoke to many people about what they looked for in a new car. Price, style, size, and brand name all played a big role. "A Mercedes tells people I am successful. A BMW says that I am going somewhere."

When we began speaking to children, we noticed something new. We asked a young boy what his favorite brand of car was and he very quickly told us "Toyota." He told us everything he knew about the Prius and its hybrid engine. He knew Toyota was pioneering environmentally friendly cars, and for that reason it was his favorite.

There are huge opportunities for brands coming into China to win the hearts of the Chinese people. They won't do it by concentrating on statistics or eyeing their wallets. They will succeed by considering what they can do to help make China a better place. The Chinese people are beginning to realize that their purchase behavior will affect the environmental future of their country, and that they will need to spend wisely to ensure that they can make a clean start.

Our Favorite Child

He traveled with his mother, father, and grandparents. It was their family vacation: one week, traveling down the brown and dirty Yangtze, sharing a cabin with four other families. He would find us every day to teach us new games and make us laugh until it hurt to smile.

Early one morning when the sun was rising, he found me on the front deck of the boat typing on my laptop. He wanted to show me that he knew the alphabet and spent an hour happily typing the letters and numbers in order, on top of the work I was doing. He practiced his English with me, and he would repeat his words in Chinese for me to learn.

Finally he ran off, pointing to me and stamping his feet on the deck repeatedly to indicate that he wanted me to stay and not go anywhere. When he returned he had his grandmother with him. He'd dragged her out of bed. He wanted to show her his new computer skills and that he could speak English. He wanted to show her that he was not only paying attention in his English class, but that he could now manage to have a conversation with a Westerner.

The conversation was very one sided. His English was far better than my Chinese. He has never stepped foot outside of China, and yet I had spent over seven years there.

"It's very dirty. It's not the Yangtze River. It is more like the Yellow River now. We make it dirty now, but someday we will have to make it clean again."

"When I grow up I want to be a top government official and catch bad people who steal, cheat, and dump garbage."

" I want a little boat I can drive up and down the river. I will clean it. I will stop China from getting dirtier. "

Xploring isn't a hard science or a preplanned process.

As soon as you begin to add statistics and structure, you lose the thing that makes Xploring real. Saatchi & Saatchi's success in China has come as a result of its willingness to embrace Xploring as a bona fide market research practice.

Keep your team small. When you take four or five people into someone's home, things become scripted and invasive. By keeping your team small, you gain intimacy. People stay real, expressing who they are as human beings, not respondents.

Two of our strongest campaigns resulted directly from Xploring.

> **"Only through participation and sharing can we be 1.3 billion times stronger. This is the power of the Internet."**

**The power of the Internet.
The power of exchange.**

The ideas brief behind the NetEase campaign "Power to the People." The campaign focuses on bringing the people of China and the world together through the Internet.

NetEase

NetEase is a Chinese Internet portal. Like all Internet companies they were fighting desperately for their share of the thriving Internet marketplace. They came to us with very clear objectives:

1. They wanted to be seen as the largest, most successful portal in China.

2. They wanted to be positioned as being very local to counteract the global strategy of international players like Yahoo and AOL.

They believed that if they were to succeed they needed to present themselves as being big.

We were spending quite a bit of time hanging around Internet cafés, watching kids talk to their friends online in Australia, Germany, or Japan and listening to their conversations. We chatted with them over Coca-Cola about the explosion of Internet technology in China, and the changes it had made to their lives.

NetEase print ad, Dragon Dance: "What if holidays were celebrated by one?"

NetEase print ad, Dragon Boat:
"What if you have to face challenges all by yourself?"

NetEase print ad, Great Wall:
"What if the Great Wall was built by one?"

NetEase print ad, Cannon Ball:
"What if no one knows the use of gunpowder?"

When we talked to them about positioning NetEase as a big player in Internet technology, they laughed. To them NetEase was one of the original portals, and was seen as being older, dated, and not as switched-on as the bigger international companies. It was good, reliable, but not exciting. We stopped talking about NetEase and started talking to them about the technology that companies like NetEase were delivering.

They felt there was no power in the technology itself, because it was always changing, growing, and adapting. Instead, they believed that power comes from the way you use technology, a fundamental belief that our client shared.

We realized that if we could get 1.3 billion people in China using NetEase technology, the entire country would benefit. It would become stronger, it would achieve more, and it would succeed. All we had to do was give power to the people.

After one month of airing our first NetEase "Power to the People" commercial, 70.3 percent of home Internet users in China had visited the NetEase site, a 39 percent increase over the previous month. Brand awareness tripled, and registered users were up by 57 percent.

Before the campaign, NetEase was seen as the number three Internet portal in China. After the campaign it was ranked as the leading Internet portal with the highest number of daily page views.

NetEase got there not because they pounded their chest and claimed to be big, the front runner, or even local. NetEase got there because they took the time to determine what people care about.

UNICEF

UNICEF is a fantastic organization that makes a real difference in the lives of thousands of children in need of healthcare and education. Like many of our clients, UNICEF came to us with the story of what they had achieved so far. If they were to continue making a real difference they needed to gain awareness not only with the public at large, but also with the Chinese government.

The typical ad for UNICEF would include needy children, a few scenes of kids in a classroom, kids being fed, and kids receiving medical attention. All of this was good, but we knew it would not meet UNICEF's objective of raising awareness further.

Our idea came one day when we were walking in the streets of Wuhan. A young girl selling roses approached me for money. You should never give money to street kids, but as I was missing my own children, I instinctively reached for the loose change in my pocket. Within seconds I was surrounded by 15 or 20 children, clinging to my clothes and pleading for money.

Our van's driver instantly began shooing them away. He picked up stones and started throwing them at the kids. They were around the same age as

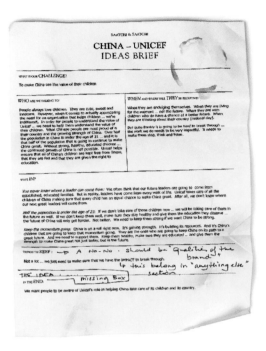

The value of children.

The ideas brief behind the award winning television commercial, "Someone Else's Child."

Gaining awareness with the public and the Chinese government.

Stills from the television commercial, "Someone Else's Child."

Someone else's child will supply food to your family.
Someone else's child will pave the roads you walk on.
Someone else's child will take you to work everyday.
Someone else's child will protect you from danger.
Someone else's child will save your life.
Someone else's child is even prepared to die for you.
All they need is a chance...to grow up like yours.

my children and the driver's children. He and I had spent hours talking about our families, yet he was treating these children like animals.

This situation helped us realize that we could not make a difference for UNICEF unless we helped people think about children differently. While we all love our own children, we are often ambivalent to other people's kids, and in particular needy kids. If UNICEF was going to be a success, they needed people to realize that every day, someone else's child has an impact on their life.

We produced a television commercial for UNICEF using as much stock footage as we could.

For the first twenty seconds there is not a single child in the commercial: just adults. We remind the viewer that these adults are all other people's children, and that they have an impact on our lives every day.

The commercial was very successful. It was shown more than three thousand times at prime time on over 300 Chinese TV stations, all at minimal cost to the client. It won the gold at the Asian Marketing Awards, a Gold Pencil at One Show and it received extensive coverage in the region on multiple communication programs.

Closing

An Xplorer must be genuine. Though the team and I traveled with clipboards and video cameras, we never hid behind them. We were ready to drop them at a moment's notice, to cook dinner with people, to sleep on the floor, and to become a part of people's lives.

A genuine Xplorer never switches off. Xploring is relentless. We bought dinner for new friends every night, bought drinks for people after their work day, and would talk to people constantly. If a person decides to be honest with you, you need to fit your circumstances around them, and to make yourself available to hear the insights that they want to share.

The numbers only tell you part of the story. They give you knowledge. When you Xplore you go beyond knowledge and you begin to understand. Xploring gives you the power to stand up in front of a client with your hand on your heart and say: this I know is true. Xploring gives you the power to speak about people—your friends—with conviction.

I have learned that as the people of China continue to gain confidence and discover more and more of the world, they will experience success on a scale never dreamed possible, and their ambition and their pride will deepen.

China isn't waiting for the world to set the pace of growth. They are setting their own pace. Not only because of what Deng Xiaoping has done, or because of what the current government is doing, but because they want to and because they can.

Their desires and their dreams are infinite. Their ambition will make China successful.

It will be increasingly harder for the world's biggest brands and most powerful companies to conquer China. Success will not be fueled by size, wealth, or even reputation.

It will be achieved through passion and ambition. And right now there is plenty of both in China.

To compete as a foreign brand, you need to look beyond the statistics and take the time to understand the people. You need to connect with them through their desires and to help fuel their ambition. You need to understand the individual who will ultimately choose your product over others.

It is the individual, their passion and their love for your brand, that will ultimately guarantee your success. If you take the time to Xplore, to get to know them and to understand them, they will reward you for it.

Acknowledgements

Many people have contributed to this book. Heidi Zhang has Xplored more miles than any one else on the team. She fearlessly approached strangers and willingly knocked on unknown doors. Dean Sciole is an Xplorer extraordinaire, constantly bringing new insights and fresh ideas to the table through his spontaneity and energy. Sahar Shaker, Sean Boyle, Danny Logue, Julien Lapka, Rock Yan, Eva Ng, and Sandy Burns have willingly put on a backpack and a pair of sneakers in search of greater understanding. Gerald Yeung, our summer intern, had the unenviable task of translating untold hours of interviews.

The photography in this book is only a small selection of the people that Chien-min Chung has captured with his lens. The high visual quality of this book is thanks to his work. Chien's innate photographic talent has seen his images appear on the cover of *Time Asia* and *Newsweek*.

Finally we must say thank you to Saatchi & Saatchi, in particular the CEOs of the Asia Pacific region, who trusted us to get on with the job any way we saw fit.

© Riley Snelling

Sandy Thompson has been a strategic planner in the ideas and advertising business for 20 years, of which 13 have been with Saatchi & Saatchi. She worked with Saatchi & Saatchi Canada before transferring to Asia, where she was Planning Director across 12 different markets. Today, she is Planning Director of Saatchi & Saatchi New York and Canada.

Sandy believes that knowledge is nothing without understanding. To understand, you need to get out from behind your desk, out from behind the one-way viewing mirrors, and instead spend some time in the real world. If you want to understand how a lion hunts, you don't go to the zoo, you go to the jungle.

Sandy and her teenage children Riley and Brin reside just outside of Toronto, but have the pleasure of enjoying the energy, pace, and excitement of New York City each and every week.

Chien-min Chung is a New York–educated photographer, currently based in Asia. He has made bodies of work on subjects as varied as child labor in Afghanistan, rural healthcare in China, and football.

His award-winning photographs have appeared on the covers of *Newsweek* and *Time Asia*. His goal as a photographer is to highlight the emotional connections between human beings through common stories and experiences, regardless of cultural and economic differences.

One in a Billion
Xploring the New World of China

© 2006 Saatchi & Saatchi
Text © 2006 Sandy Thompson
Photographs © 2006 Chien-min Chung
Foreword © 2006 Tom Peters

All rights reserved. No part of this book may be reproduced in any manner in any media, or transmitted by any means whatsoever, electronic or mechanical (including photocopy, film or video recording, Internet posting, or any other information storage and retrieval system), without the prior written permission of the publisher.

Published in the United States by powerHouse Books,
a division of powerHouse Cultural Entertainment, Inc.
37 Main Street, Brooklyn, NY 11201-1021
telephone 212 604 9074, fax 212 366 5247
e-mail: info@powerHouseBooks.com
website: www.powerHouseBooks.com

First edition, 2006

Library of Congress Cataloging-in-Publication Data:

Thompson, Sandy, 1963–
    One in a billion : Xploring the New World of China / by Sandy Thompson.
        p. cm.
    ISBN 1-57687-296-3 (hardcover)
      1. Marketing research--China. 2. Consumers--China--Attitudes. 3. National characteristics, Chinese.
      4. China--Civilization. 5. China--Economic conditions--2000- 6. China--Social conditions--2000- I. Title.

    HF5415.2.T475 2005
    658.8'34'0951--dc22

                                                              2005014667

Hardcover ISBN 1-57687-296-3

Printed and bound by Pimlico Book International, Hong Kong

Book design by Mine Suda

A complete catalog of powerHouse Books and Limited Editions is available upon request; please call, write, or Xplore our website.

10 9 8 7 6 5 4 3 2 1

Printed and bound in China

www.Xploring.com

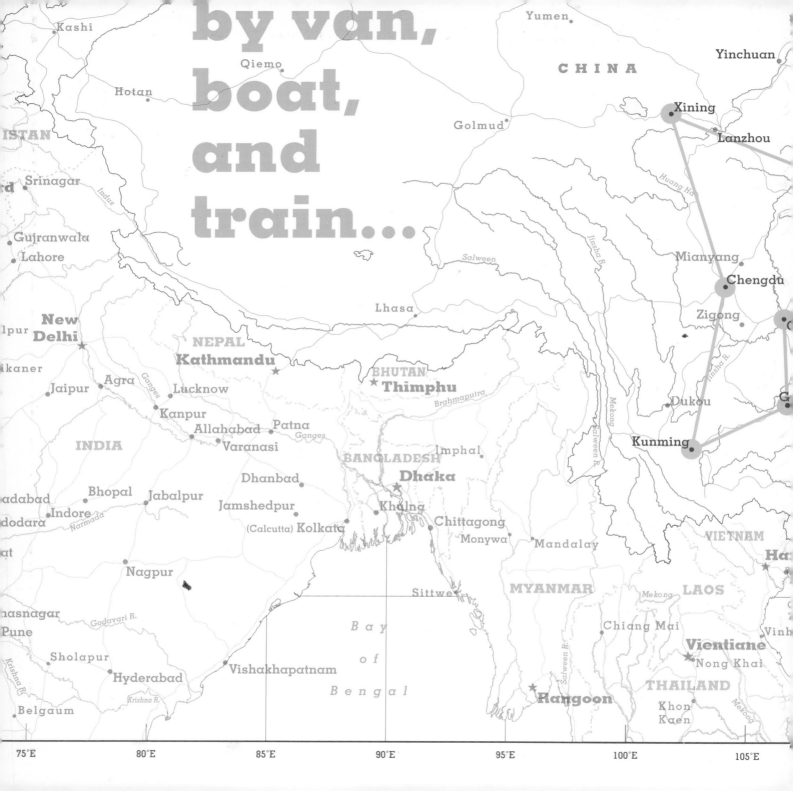